A DORLING KINDERSLEY BOOK

Conceived, edited, and designed by DK Direct Limited

Note to parents

What's Inside? Great Inventions is designed to help young children understand the workings of some of the world's important inventions. It shows why a sewing machine needs two threads to make a stitch, how sound is transmitted by a telephone, and what makes the sparks to fire a flintlock gun. It is a book for you and your child to read and talk about together, and to enjoy.

Editor Hilary Hockman
Designer John Strange
Typographic Designer Nigel Coath
U.S. Editor Laaren Brown

Illustrators Ray Hutchins/Linden Artists,
Barry Robson/Linden Artists, Steve Weston/Linden Artists
Photographers Ralph Hall, Kevin Mallett
Written by Alexandra Parsons
Consultant John Farndon
Design Director Ed Day
Editorial Director Jonathan Reed

Additional photography by Dave King

First American Edition, 1993

10 9 8 7 6 5 4 3 2 1

Published in the United States by
Dorling Kindersley, Inc., 232 Madison Avenue
New York, New York 10016

Library of Congress Cataloging-in-Publication Data
Great Inventions. – 1st American ed.
    p. cm. – (What's inside?)
    Summary: Examines the origins of eight inventions, including the telephone,
flushing toilet, and printing press, and explains how they work.
    ISBN 1-56458-220-5
    1. Inventions – Miscellanea – Juvenile literature.
[1. Inventions. 2. Technology.] I. Series.
T48.I52 1993
620 — dc20   92-54273 CIP AC

Printed in Italy

WHAT'S INSIDE?
GREAT
INVENTIONS

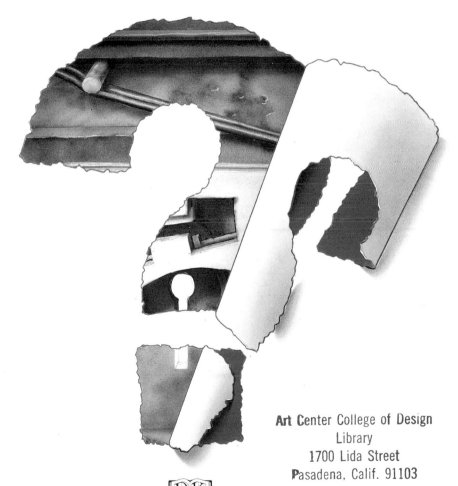

DK

DORLING KINDERSLEY
LONDON • NEW YORK • STUTTGART

LOCK

Locks and keys made of wood and metal have been around for thousands of years. They were used in ancient China and ancient Egypt. In 1778, a British engineer called Robert Barron invented the lever lock.

This beautifully decorated brass lever lock, made for an inside door, is about 100 years old.

The latch slots into the door frame to keep the door shut. It is pulled out of the door frame when the handle is turned.

The door handle operates the latch.

The key goes in here to operate the bolt.

The bolt locks and unlocks the door. It fits into the door frame, too.

The key has a cut-out step pattern. It will fit only the lock it was made for.

A combination bike lock works
like a lever lock. Inside the lock are
some levers, holding on to a bolt.
When all the levers are lined up,
the bolt slips free.

These are little metal plates,
or levers. Each lever is a
different size. They match
the steps cut out in the key.

The levers hold this bolt
pin in place, and the bolt
pin holds the bolt in place.

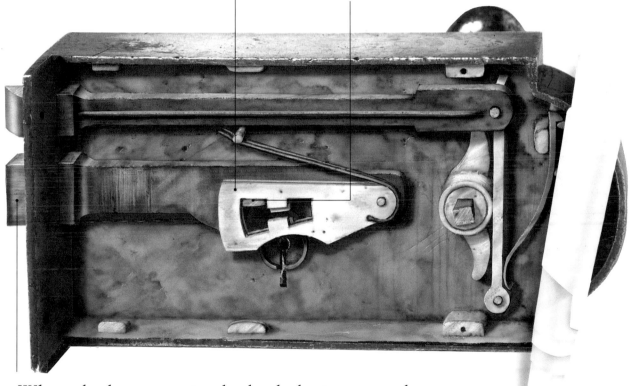

When the key turns in the keyhole, it moves the
levers and frees the bolt pin so the bolt can move.
The bolt moves away from the door frame to
unlock the door, and into the door frame to lock it.

SEWING MACHINE

Before the sewing machine was invented, clothes were all hand-made. You either stitched your own or, if you were rich enough, had them made to order. You couldn't just rush out and buy a new outfit. All that changed in 1851 when Isaac Singer came up with a sewing machine that could be used in factories and in homes.

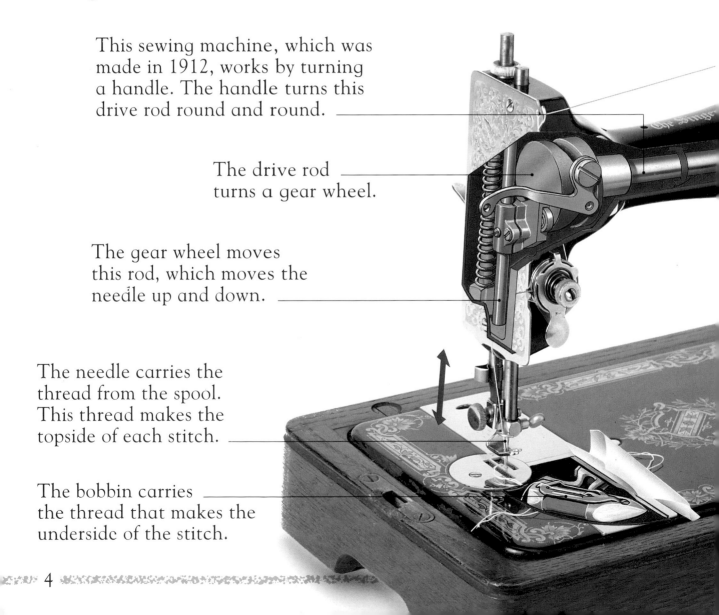

This sewing machine, which was made in 1912, works by turning a handle. The handle turns this drive rod round and round.

The drive rod turns a gear wheel.

The gear wheel moves this rod, which moves the needle up and down.

The needle carries the thread from the spool. This thread makes the topside of each stitch.

The bobbin carries the thread that makes the underside of the stitch.

The bobbin thread gets looped around the needle thread to make the complete stitch, top and bottom.

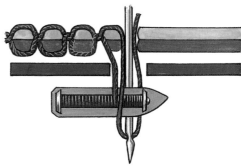

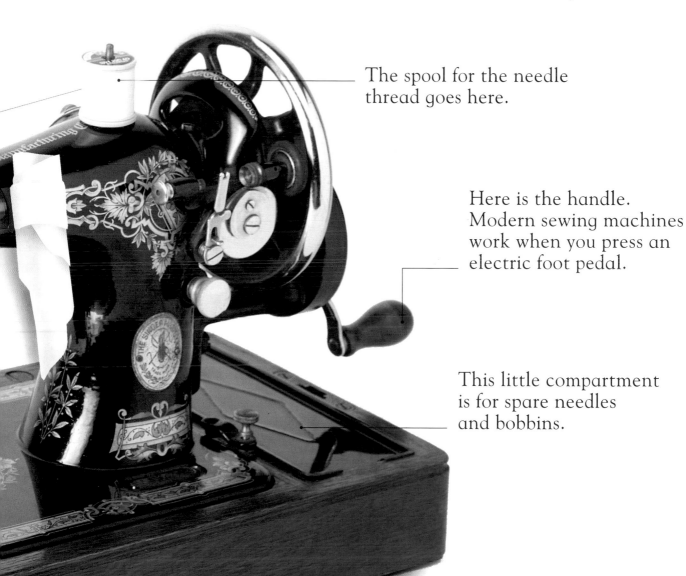

The spool for the needle thread goes here.

Here is the handle. Modern sewing machines work when you press an electric foot pedal.

This little compartment is for spare needles and bobbins.

TELEPHONE

On March 10, 1876, Alexander Graham Bell made the first telephone call, from one room in his house to another. Both Bell's mother and wife were deaf, and Bell had been interested in sound for many years.

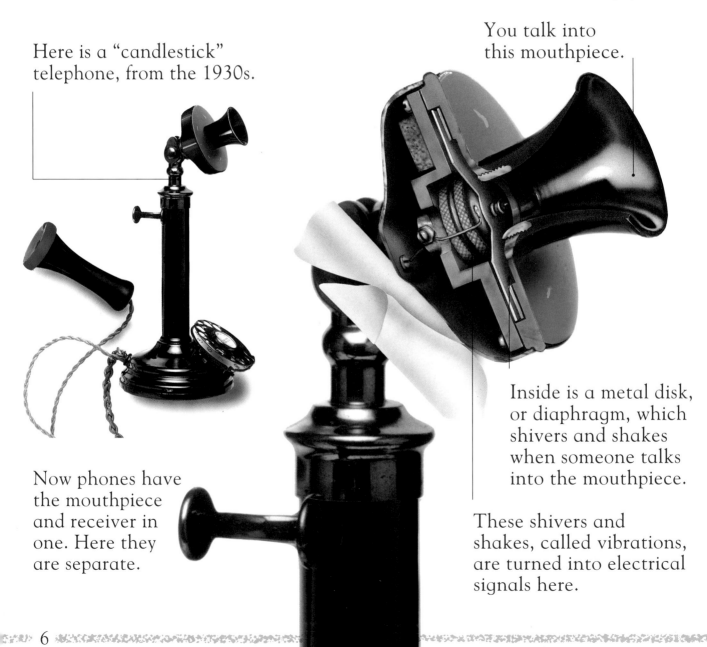

Here is a "candlestick" telephone, from the 1930s.

You talk into this mouthpiece.

Inside is a metal disk, or diaphragm, which shivers and shakes when someone talks into the mouthpiece.

Now phones have the mouthpiece and receiver in one. Here they are separate.

These shivers and shakes, called vibrations, are turned into electrical signals here.

Make your own "phone" with two empty plastic yogurt cups. Join them with a piece of string knotted through the bases. You make the container shiver and shake with the vibrations of your voice. The vibrations pass down the string (but only if the string is tight) and into the other cup.

The electrical signals pass down the wire, then along special cables into the receiver of the person you are calling.

This is the receiver, where you listen.

Here the electrical signals turn this electric magnet on and off.

The ons and offs of the electric magnet make a diaphragm in the receiver shiver and shake.

These vibrations make a sound come out of the receiver – a sound just like the one that went in the mouthpiece of the caller's telephone.

FLINTLOCK PISTOL

The first guns were cannons – tubes packed with gunpowder.
A cannonball was loaded into the open end and the powder was lit.
The gunpowder exploded, and the ball shot out. The first hand-held guns, called pistols, worked in much the same way. Flintlock pistols were invented over 350 years ago. They had a built-in flint to make the sparks that light the powder.

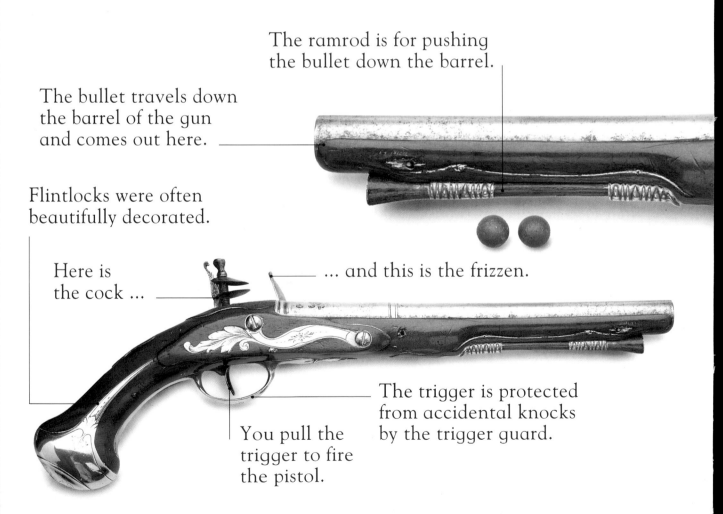

The ramrod is for pushing the bullet down the barrel.

The bullet travels down the barrel of the gun and comes out here.

Flintlocks were often beautifully decorated.

Here is the cock ...

... and this is the frizzen.

The trigger is protected from accidental knocks by the trigger guard.

You pull the trigger to fire the pistol.

Like the old flintlock, a toy cap gun
uses gunpowder – but only a little!

A piece of flint is gripped
in the cock. Flint is a very
hard stone that makes
sparks if it is struck against
a rough metal surface.

The frizzen has a rough metal surface.
When the trigger is pulled, the flint
rubs against the frizzen and sparks fly.

The flint pushes the frizzen forward.
This uncovers a little pan of special firing
powder that is set alight by the sparks.

A flame shoots through
this little hole in the pan ...

... and sets fire to
the gunpowder.

The gunpowder explodes
and fires the bullet.

RADIO

In 1887, Heinrich Hertz discovered that a big electric spark sends out invisible waves of electricity called radio waves. They travel so fast, they could go around the earth seven times in one second. In 1894, Guglielmo Marconi had the idea of using radio waves to send electrical messages, and it worked!

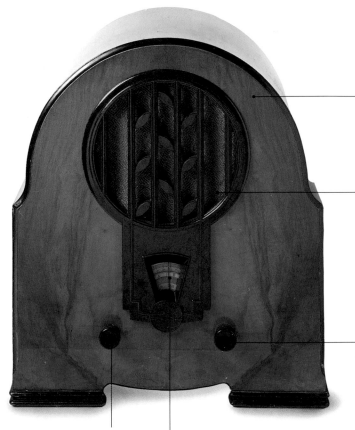

Many radios were built like pieces of furniture. This model, finished in walnut, was made in 1933.

The sounds come out of the loudspeaker, which is behind this fabric grille.

This knob is for tuning in to different radio waves that carry different radio programs.

This is the on/off knob.

The dial shows which station the tuner has found.

This is probably the smallest radio in the world. Valves have now been replaced by tiny silicon chips, and the antennas are tucked away inside.

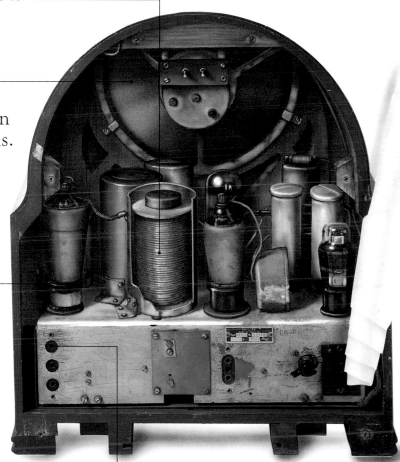

The tuner picks up different stations from these coils, depending on how far along the coil it is.

The loudspeaker has a membrane – a sort of drumhead – that is shaken up by the electrical signals. The shaking of the membrane makes the sounds we hear.

Valves are tubes that make the little electrical signals stronger.

The antenna wire plugs in here. When the radio waves reach the antenna wire, they are turned into little electrical signals.

FLUSH TOILET

The flush toilet was first invented in 1589. It didn't catch on because there weren't any drains to take away the dirty water. A hundred years ago, when many houses had running water and were connected to sewers, toilets were reinvented, and they looked like this.

Here is the cistern that holds the water that flushes the waste down the toilet.

Pull the china handle to flush the toilet.

The seat is made of wood. It is always warm to sit on.

Water flushes into the bowl from under this rim.

The bowl is made of decorated china.

This part is called the U-bend. Dirty water is forced through it and along to the drains by the flushing action.

Toilet paper was invented in 1857, but for a long time it was a luxury. People made do with old newspapers and shopping catalogs!

The chain pulls this lever down ...

... and the end of the lever pulls this cylinder up, so the water in the cistern is sucked quickly through the downpipe to flush the bowl.

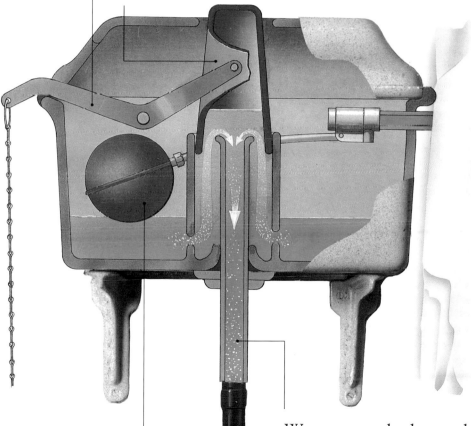

When the cistern is empty and the ball valve is down, water pours in to refill the cistern.

Water travels down this pipe from the cistern to the bowl.

PHONOGRAPH

The phonograph was the first machine that could record and play back sounds. It was invented in 1877 by Thomas Edison. For this phonograph, made in 1898, the sounds were recorded on grooved waxed cylinders.

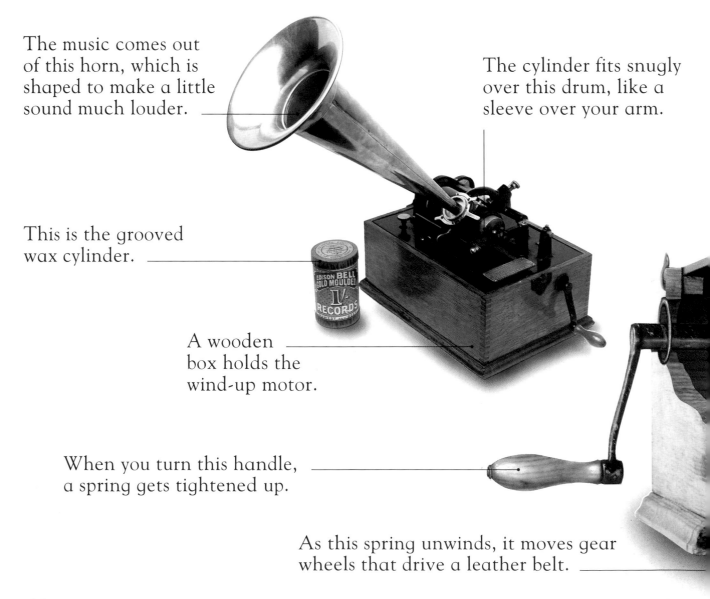

The music comes out of this horn, which is shaped to make a little sound much louder.

The cylinder fits snugly over this drum, like a sleeve over your arm.

This is the grooved wax cylinder.

A wooden box holds the wind-up motor.

When you turn this handle, a spring gets tightened up.

As this spring unwinds, it moves gear wheels that drive a leather belt.

Turn the key to play a music box. The spring unwinding inside turns a drum with spikes, and as the drum turns, the spikes twang little metal strips. These make the noise you hear.

The needle sends its shivers and shakes onto a tiny disk in here, which vibrates. This bounces air up and down to make the sound we hear through the horn.

A steel needle rides along the turning cylinder, shivering and shaking as it runs over the bumps in the grooves.

The horn fits here.

The leather belt makes the drum go round and round. The drum and cylinder turn together.

PRINTING PRESS

Until Johannes Gutenberg invented the printing press nearly 550 years ago, books had to be copied out by hand, and only the rich could afford them. Gutenberg's printing press, with movable type, was one of the most important inventions ever. It meant that books – with all the knowledge and ideas they hold – were cheaper for everyone.

First, the printer gets the letters to make the words. Metal letters are made in molds and stuck onto little wooden blocks. The letters – or type – are backward.

The blocks of type have to be put together line by line, in a metal tray, to make up a form.

A form holds one page of type.

The printer spreads special printing ink over the form, then lays a piece of paper over the inked form.

Print your own pictures! Cut a raised design into a halved potato (cut away the parts you don't want), dip the potato in paint, and press the design onto paper.

This hinged section – or tympan – is folded down over the form and the paper.

The tympan, form, and paper are pushed under this heavy weight.

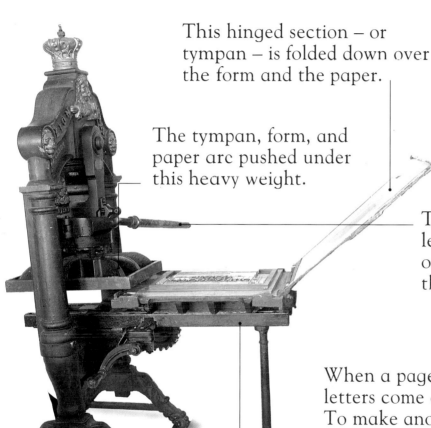

The printer lowers the lever to press the paper onto the inky letters of the form.

When a page has been printed, the letters come out the right way around. To make another copy, the printer re-inks the form and repeats the process. When the ink is dry, the pages are stitched together to make a book.

This press was built in 1866.

It took Gutenberg three years to make and set up all the type for his first book, the Bible. He printed 200 copies in 1456.

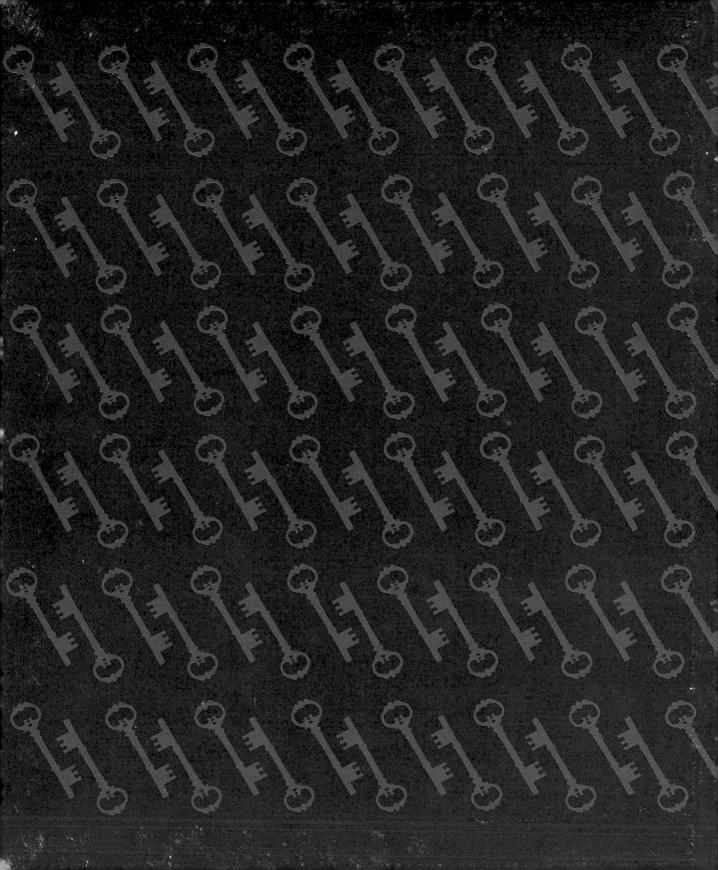